# Coulda Bin Summin

# Coulda Bin Summin

## Mike Jenkins

Planet

First published
in Wales in 2001
by Planet

PO Box 44
Aberystwyth
Ceredigion SY23 3ZZ
Cymru/Wales

Cover design: Glyn Rees

Printed by Gwasg Gomer
Llandysul, Ceredigion

Published with the financial support
of the Arts Council of Wales

ISBN 0 9505188 9 1

To my friends and comrades in The Red Poets' Society

## Acknowledgements

Some of these poems first appeared in *Poetry Wales, Planet, Chasing the Dragon, Roundyhouse, New Welsh Review, Y Faner Goch, Red Poets' Society,* Wilfred Owen Society *Newsletter* and anthology, *In the Spirit of Wilfred Owen, The Western Mail, WTBF!, Slope, Red Lamp, Drawing Down the Moon,* BBC Wales.

# Contents

| | |
|---|---|
| Shop Boyz | 1 |
| Anon Sloopy | 2 |
| Day A-Duchess Come | 3 |
| Train-Time | 5 |
| The Jesus T-Shirt | 7 |
| Fochriw Airport | 8 |
| Suckin Up t' the Right People | 9 |
| Big Mick | 10 |
| Free Willy | 11 |
| Work Experience | 12 |
| Carboy | 13 |
| Till-a Truth | 14 |
| Green Eggs | 16 |
| When-a Wind Blew Black | 17 |
| Cause for Concern | 18 |
| Jezzie | 19 |
| Operation Albania | 20 |
| Krayzee Gang | 21 |
| Down-a Shops | 22 |
| Nothin Like Princess Di | 24 |
| Time is Dribbling Away | 25 |
| Gwyn Alf | 27 |
| Carn Take Theyr Beer | 29 |
| Spider in-a Bright Light | 30 |
| Signing f'ra Circus | 32 |
| Matchstick Man | 33 |
| Mad Jack Spoils V.E. Day | 34 |
| Too Ol at Forty | 37 |
| Look at Istree | 38 |
| A Ready Torture | 39 |
| Grim Reaper of-a Factree | 40 |
| Another Bleedin Tear | 41 |

All Ail Ower Bran' New System     43
Waitin t' Be Robbed     45
Coulda Bin Summin     47
People Yew Don' See     51
New Age Riot     52
Banned     54
Soap Star     55
Passion Fruit     56
Jitterbug Jade     58
The Big Ole     59
No Fashion on a Plate     60
Smelly Shelly     62
Trolley Push     63

SHOP BOYZ

Them boyz, them shop boyz
they'll skank yewr breath,
yew got any glass eyes
they'll ave em f' ball-bearin's,
they'll ave yewr gran's dentures
an make em inta lock-picks.
They'll ave yewr wigs
t' keep theyr Rottweilers
nice 'n' cosy at night,
yewr aunty's Woman's Own t' roll
out giant spliffs with.
If yew d'go by bike
make shewer yew chain it
t' yewr legs or else...
an if yew d' go by car
make shewer-a rust's so bard
it falls apart arfta 30 miles-p'r-ower.
Don' park yewr baby-buggy
f' more 'an 10 seconds
or yew'll find little Lisa
rollin with all-a coke cans.
They'll tax yewr boots
t' ewse as flower-pots,
yewr tooth-braces t' dust
theyr knuckles with.
Them boyz, them shop boyz
with baseball caps an baseball bats:
even-a pigs give up
when 'ey ram-raided Raji's
with-a ten ton truck.
They'd ave yewr flesh
t' skin up, if 'ey could find
knives 'at were sharp enough.

## ANON SLOOPY

Int no karaoke croakalong,
int no stand-up juke box
"We wan' Bard Company, Floyd, Endrix!"

Ewsed t' sing with my back
t' the audience.
Ewsed t' let em
gasp at my cheek!
Now we got ower own mewsic:
rap metal blues rock.
Pubs've wound us up
arf way through a mulin set:
"Sorry boyz, too loud, no tewns...
mind, I ewsed t' be inta Led Zep."

We even played-a fancy Cooler Club
an done ower pisstake
livin-fera-weekend
jobs-make-em-brain-dead song.
An guess wha? All-a max factrees
clapped along, so cool
'ey sweated four layers down.

We'll be famous one day
f' bein unknown: The NeverAsBins
make it with a single "Anon Sloopy, Sloopy Anon."

## DAY A-DUCHESS COME

We ad a visit off-a Duchess o' Gloucester
(someone sayz she's arf German)
nobody's ever yeard of er before,
some cousin 20 times over
of-a bloody Queen.

The whool week the Eads wuz ravin,
never seen em in-a corridors
s' much time. Thin's woz done
what ad bin waitin f' years:
pot-oles on-drive filled in
jest before Tower miners appeared.

The Big Ead's muriel by-a stairs
ad its swastika scrubbed off
(las time it woz WANKER
right across is slapper).
Ev'ry little scuff woz touched up
an-a foyer woz like Kew Gardens.
A-deputy Miss Price woz up-a ladder
rubbin-a windows frantic.

She come by elicopter landin
on ower so-called tennis courts
(no markin's, no nets, no nothin).
More pigs 'an Cardiff v. Swansea.
There wuz a posh limo t' take er
up-a drive, red carpet an choir ready
an all-a swots sittin f' owers writin.

We woz stuck in-a room watchin
*When Saturday Comes* mega-brill swearin
an shaggin. Oo is she anyway,

what ave she ever done?
Presented er with-a miner's lamp 'ey did,
I'd-a give er worse 'an a gun.

## TRAIN-TIME

Kick the cans
oo's gunna win?
shaven-eaded rugby fans
train-time train-time

Knock it back
get it down
oo's gunna be
ev'ryone's clown?

Sittin on-a platform
frayed coat 'n' shoes
gazin at-a brochures
bright oliday ues

Couple on-a floor
low as yew cun get
"Any spare cash mister?"
still jokin wet

There's a cheer from-a park
there's coal on-a line
there's boyz ud go anywhere
train-time train-time

Announcer with a posh voice
an a lipshine load
women with bags an kids
pullin to an fro

Steppin through-a doorways
steppin on-a scales
the weight an the distance
an arrow never fails

Yew cun bring ome-a feathers
t' make yew look fine
while-a pigeons 're pickin
train-time train-time.

# THE JESUS T- SHIRT

The nice young man on-a train
ad JESUS CHRIST cross-a top
of is T-shirt, never thought
youngsters nowadays ud care s' much
an ee seemed awful rough,
adn' shaved f' days,
but still ower Lord ad a beard.

Is girl didn seem s' weird,
all dressed in black,
goin to a fewnral p'raps?
Mind, er lipstick were purple
an she looked awful pale
like she wuz goin t' be sick.

They did seem very close,
reminded me o' my courtin days.
Spect ee do take some flak
f' bein so oly... good f'r im, I say.

An then in Cardiff ee got up.
Couldn believe my eyes
JESUS IS A C...
couldn bring myself t' read,
blood an a demon on is sleeve!
I give im such a look.
Devil-worshippers in broad daylight!
Strolled off and-in-and.
If I woz is mam,
wouldn make rags from that.

## FOCHRIW AIRPORT

Well, we woz drivin over t' Deri
jest f'ra stroll in-a countree park,
when I seen em... course, I've yeard
plenty o' jokes 'bout Fochriw Airport.

Sure nuff stuff... real as eather,
an aeroplane an then, another.
Fochriw Airport does exist,
not jest a story f' bullshit artists.

Course, it's f' model planes
an it's nowhere near the village,
but ow far's Cardiff Airport
from all-a arcades an precincts?

Thought of folk the size o' digits
queuin by the lake... well, pond,
t' board flights f' glorious Bargoed
an-a Costa C'philly beyond.

## SUCKIN UP T' THE RIGHT PEOPLE

Der! course I 'member er!
Back of-a Kirk'ouse night club
an in-a bus-shelter
givin loadsa BJ's,
blowin em boyz out proper.
We ewsed t' say
she always chose vanilla.

She woz 'n expert mind,
on'y time she'd stop talkin,
more ead than a pint o' Guinness.
If there'd bin a BJ sprint
f' Wales in-a 'lympics
she'd-a left ev'ryone be'ind.

Now she's a bloody councillor,
I seen er face in-a paper
(I yeard she've met Tony Blair).
Carn believe ow she've got on,
all-a boyz slagged er off no end,
but still queued up f' one!
P'raps all-a time she wuz practisin
in case she ever met Clinton.

BIG MICK

When-a cops ganged in
an arrested a boy f' swearin
Big Mick ee sayz "Old it,
ee int a piece o' shit!"

Big Mick wuz 32 an baldin,
a skin with Bluebirds flyin
over is ands 'n' arms:
wern fulla aggro, ad gentle charms.

Before ee ad time t' tell-a feds
ee tended kids in ospital beds
an didn give no-one a lampin
'less 'ey come f'r im tampin:

ee felt a single blow to is ead,
sky disappeared, thought ee wuz dead,
till ee come round in a cell
is lump killin like ee woke in ell.

"Wha ave I done? Int done nothin!"
"Put it like this... assaulting a policeman...
six witnesses to prove it... all in uniform."
Big Mick wuz fulla rage an scorn,

ee coulda kicked-a cop's smug features
like a ball, like all them teachers
oo'd always called im thick,
but ee jest muttered "Fuckin pricks!"

Ee wuz throbbin worse 'an any angover,
thoughts of is job wen' over 'n' over:
ee'd bin t' Carlisle, away t' Spain,
but ee'd never go t' bleedin Ull again.

# FREE WILLY

I know this fella, see,
went t' Voodoo Videos t' take out Free Willy
thinkin it were a cock film:
wanted t' turn on is new girlfriend.

Well, they seen it together
cwtched up on-a sofa
an... yew know wha?... aye!
there wuz tricks in er eyes.

"Wanna bath?" she sayz "an we'll play Orcas."
"Okay," ee replies, "jes get my rubber ducklin's."
So fulla foam an bubblin
ee wuz dyin t' ave er in-a water.

They dived in like a coupla seals
so ee carn believe it's real,
it on'y appens in films
starrin Brando or Oliver Reed.

Ee neally pissed isself
ee wuz so thrilled,
till she grabs old o' is ol boy
an squeezes it like some baby's toy.

"Ey! Wha yew doin? Watch yewr nails!"
"Didn yew feel my arpoon?
This one's called The Revenge of the Whale."
Ee thought, "P'raps I shoulda bought er a lovespoon."

## WORK EXPERIENCE

I wuz up the Oochie,
(or Atchetland, as they say)
workin f'ra Council.

Workin? Tha's a larf!
We mos'ly done boardin up,
the ouses woz mankin
with masses o' rats lodgin.

The flats ad doors arf-angin
like teeth droppin out
an windows with cracks
taped up like lightnin,
some walls an ceilin's
wuz decorated with mushrooms.

Oh aye, I learnt a lot
in them three days before
I wuz kicked out f' messin.
Anyway, I done em a favour
smokin out all them vermin.

I woz a trainee arsonist,
I got some morals, see.
Always put it out with piss!

CARBOY

Carboy's gonna get me
an I don' know why.
Coulda looked im in the eyes,
coulda met is ex-girl,
coulda breathed in is terrortree,
coulda tol someone ee's a druggie.
Carboy's gotta knife
an now so ave I.
I gotta, in I?
It's on'y f' protection —
if ee come f' me
I'll let im ave it, see
(flicknife smuggled through customs
down my jeans like 'n ard-on).
Carboy's got s' many friends
(they're arselickers really),
I need t' ave it by me,
elps me walk tidy,
though night puts a shits up me
there's alleys an there's corners
I carn see a fuckin thin.
Carboy'll do 'n an'brake turn
an run me down like a dopey sheep,
like a shitty rabbit shocked
in-a eadlights' burn.

## TILL-A TRUTH

I know I done wrong
nickin off-a shops down town,
phets an maz no end,
carryin on beyond
with arf o' my friends' men,
but I never done
what I'm in yer for.

Sometimes all I do is scream
out-a window, but oo'll lissen?
Scream like a siren,
like someone oose ouse
is goin up an all
theyr precious love-ones.

Not sayin I never done arm,
bein ard's the on'y way
t' get respect round yer,
yew gotta show oo's oo
with fists o' fear.

Int a second goes by
I'm thinkin o' my kids,
ow ee's copin, ow 'ey miss
theyer mam, ev'ry night
I d' whisper to em
sif my voice woz witchin.

Darkness int day or night
no more, int summer nor winter,
int even oliday or worktime.
I think o' them pooer little ones:
all the ashes fallin, surroundin...

nightmares I'm brushin em away,
but they will stay
till-a truth takes em.

## GREEN EGGS

Ee wuz crashed out on-a desk
ead down space cadet
as always, till-a teacher says
"Pick up yewr pen, Jamie!"
an ee wakes up f'r a second
face red as bloody ketchup,
eyes like pools o' piss
an 'en ee falls agen
into is trance.
Issa green eggs, ev'ryone says...
I keep thinkin o' them atchin
in is ead, insex breedin
as ee lay, eatin away
inta is brain an poppin out
of is yers all waxy wings
undreds of em like flyin ants
on'y bright green thin's
with shiny bodies like pills
leavin is skull like 'n ollow
in a tree trunk,
bitin ev'ryone in school
s' they drop off like im.
The teachers leave im be,
it's miles easier when ee's sleepin
than creatin ell, givin em stick
or skankin anythin is ands ud pick
to pay f'r is excape.

## WHEN-A WIND BLEW BLACK

Send us all yewr bloody cack
we on'y come from Dowlais Top
we're ewsed t' crap up yer:
ad it f' yers we ave,
the boggin Opencast with more dust
'an miners' spit, sheets on-a lines
like-a tar from fags
an more noise 'an-a motorways.
But le's grovel coz 'ey give us
the Astroturf t' compensate
f'r all-a times when-a wind blew black.

Send us all yewr oily sand,
arfta all,  we got a lovely Big Ole
t' keep fillin now-a coal's ewsed up,
got more variety o' smells
than 'ey got burgers up Big Mac's,
got a species o' super-rat
eats all rubbish no matter what.

Send us yewr deadly waste,
we're ewsed t' buryin thin's, o' course,
t' coverin up the past:
we'll watch f'ra different colour smoke
risin from be'ind the wire,
we'll splutter like we always done
an mutter an protest:
they're ewsed t' ower voices by now
cuttin no metal, outin no fire.

CAUSE FOR CONCERN
(For Jazz)

I'm thick, they tell me so,
got nothin inside o' my ead
in-a bottom class of a crap school
"Yew? Wha's s' SPECIAL 'bout yew?
Yew're jest stewpid, tha's all!"

Carn spell arf o' most words.
Carn write, ink's like squashed turds.
Carn read, books like metal balls
fixed t' my lips.

Dull see, other kids poke 'n' joke,
while I gurn an make noises
like a zoo set loose.

"Hey! Answer me! What is this?"
Gimme a rod an I'll catch
yew a fish,  gimme a tree
an I'll climb it like a squirrel,
gimme paper an I'll grime it.

I'm a 0 percenter Cause For Concern
down arrow in Remove every lesson
name on-a board mos' ticks
in detention one thousand lines,
but I cun spell BITCH an BASTARD
right ev'ry fuckin time.

## JEZZIE

Round town ev'rybody knew im,
resident alkie arfta Dai Raspberry
got finlee knocked down
tryin to outbox a lorry.

Now ol Billy Sticks is left
sellin newspapers from doorways,
is "Echo!Echo!" with a mutter
jabbed at ones oo don' buy.

Jezzie's gone down at las,
ee died a coupla times before,
choked on is own puke,
come up with a roar.

Cans ad grown from is ands
is clothes woz ummin,
staggered along an swore
at is own ead's drummin.

But ee never urt no-one,
jest drunk isself silly,
till ee collapsed t' ground
in-a bus station f'r all t' see.

'ey left im tha las time
thinkin ee were sleepin agen,
in-a evenin when nobody come,
found by coppers arfta crime.

"Come on Jezzie! Yewr a disgrace!"
copper yelled, liftin is face,
is eyeballs two white stones:
from is body a bottle rolled.

## OPERATION ALBANIA

Operation Albania? Oo come up with tha one?
More like Operation Vietnam:
Apocalypse Merthyr, raids on omes
jes like on-a films.

Picked up all-a real ard cases, din'ey?
'leven year ol boy with a slug gun!
Aye, 'ey got some dealers orright,
but ow bout-a sons o' snobs tradin eroin?

Tha elicopter beam like gropin ands,
bet them cops wuz peepin toms.
We all come under-a same suspicion,
I felt guilty an I woz walkin ome!

Al-bloody-bania? Smore like N. Ireland,
reckon 'ey've borrowed all-a elicopters.
I cun see summin's gotta be done,
but crime don' come from nowhere.

All tha crime int risin
jes coz-a weather's improvin,
makin it easier f' night burglars
t' see wha they're doin.

Anyroad, we all yeard tha sound,
so people switched off-a Sky,
come inta the street, ad sweeps
on oo wuz arrested an why.

Maybe it wern tha bard arfta all,
bit of a show in the air,
if they ad guns on them machines
it ud be like a real war.

## KRAYZEE GANG

I keep well clear of-a Krayzee gang,
not jest coz I'd ave a lampin from my mam.
D'yew reckon tha theyr names come
from them two twins oo carved up London?

'ey smoke fags an swear at ev'ryone,
ride theyr bikes through ower games,
'ey stay up late till arfta one,
my dad sayz it's like Jesse James.

They're inta drugs inta ev'rythin,
my friend Dean sayz 'ey got green eggs:
down the ol Social, place like a bin,
idin be'ind-a rubble an 'n edge.

I keep 'way from-a Krayzee gang,
'ey know language worse 'an any video.
Dean sayz 'ey got knives an all,
grass em up, 'ey'll cut off yewer ands.

I seen em take stuff, white tabs,
seen em ride no ands one wheel,
seen em climb-a school roof, they're mad!
seen em go with girls f'ra feel.

My mam's warned me bout-a Krayzee gang,
but wha's all 'is bout-a marzipan?
It's on-a cakes an she don' do nothin:
Christmas won' never be the same.

## DOWN-A SHOPS

*Gis a fag*
*Gis a drag*
*Gis another chip*

Down-a shops lunchtime
litter knee-deep,
an dogs with-a runs,
pushers come up
"Ey yew, wanna trip?
Speed go mad,
green eggs lose yer ead."
Alkies faces
stars in glass,
stars of plunder
stars of ate.

*Gis a fag*
*Gis a drag*
*Gis another chip*

Gis a job sellin —
what'll it be,
tits f'r a tenner
arse f' more?
Never see-a pigs round yer,
don' care no more,
cept evenin's round benches
with theyr zero tolerance
(we move somewhere else
well away from camras).

Coz I gotta excape
this shit-ole place,

a bin I'd climb
longin t' get out,
risk the drop.

*Gis a fag*
*Gis a drag*
*Gis another chip*

## NOTHIN LIKE PRINCESS DI

Der! D'yew yer whar appened to er?
She's bein buried later —
aye, she've died ave tha Joanna,
awful crash with some ooligan joyrider.

Seen it comin f' years I did,
broke up with er usband Carl
when ee flipped is lid,
ad arf a rugby team since an all.

Tell yew wha, lucky no passers-by wuz killed,
tha foreign bloke she've bin goin with
is guts woz also spilled
an-a driver woz off of is ead.

Seen it comin, she ad no tidy job,
though people say she've done a lot
f' kids up-a Barnado's omes,
er life wuz like 'n oliday in Rome.

It's them pooer kids I feel sorry for,
she dumped em with strangers,
they ardly knew er as a mam:
too busy clubbin with er fancy man.

Clothes like a bloody princess she wore
an she talked with a proper twang,
musta made is money outside-a law:
'ey come down to earth with a bang!

I don' mean t' be sick, not me,
it's jest tha... wha with Princess Di, see?
Tha dog Joanna spoilt my day,
it int ewman t' end in tha way.

## TIME IS DRIBBLING AWAY

I read on-a bus-shelter
wishin I coulda wrote
summin tha clever.
Idin in my ood
in-a misty rain,
waitin f'r them girls
oo pass this way,
a-perms o' ferns
coverin the valley
like-a damp autumn
wouldn go away.
Up yer I'm left be'ind:
it's ard t' see-a black,
the grass 'ey planted
slike 'n astral turf.

Where 'ey goin 'en,
them two crackin girls
oo won' even turn
theyr gorgeous eads
t' where I'm unched
in my concrete coat?
The streams're dribblin
like gob on-a chin
o' some ol nutter.
In New Tredegar
a-clock's stuck on twelve,
coz time's water
mockin as it goes
t' places I'll never get t'.

I stare at theyr orsey bums:
like a whip my mate

ee rises so quick.
I fleg on-a pavement
opin 'ey'll look back.
My mate ee's solid as a brick,
won' keep still like a ferret
wants t' climb, t' get out,
while all's I do is sit.

## GWYN ALF

Never bin one f'r istree
lines o' dates
them kings an queens,
my memree no ware'ouse
f' such thin's, but ee...
ee spoke like one of us
took me back in them talks
I wandered to at first.
Ee brung it up t' date,
constructin a buildin
o' sights an smells
is stammer a-drillin
ands framin windows,
is fag the chimlee.
An oo owns 'is ouse?
ee seemed t' say.

Never bin one f' politics, mind,
them politicians on'y come
'lection time buyin ower votes,
I know enough t' know
a cross is thin as ink,
once 'ey get in
'ey'll all forget, but im...
ee wuz always from
round yer, no matter ow far
ee went, Russia or America,
ee laid a track
f' tram or train, is spinnin brain
'maginin a future town
where we'd get off, t' larf
an eat an sing under-a roof
of-a place we'd made.

Ee coughed is guts out...
death? never bin one t' say
tha much about it,
but when I yeard 'bout im
I couldn elp it,
my missis sayz, "Don' talk soft!
Yew never even knew im!"
But I felt-a cement
dryin my throat, my ead
poundin with-a wheels turnin.

## CARN TAKE THEYR BEER

Seen em there, off it,
outa theyer eads
like a Rugby Club on tour:
with a wooden prick,
toyin with it,
dippin it in froth o' stout
an lickin it off,
idin it in a girl's bag,
usin it t' play pool with.

Look at tha fool
pinchin women's bums
like ee collected em,
them ones playin maginree guitar
an singin darft songs
oose words go "Duh ra duh ra duh..."

See em fightin like closin time,
one woman leapin on-a back t' stop,
like bullies in-a yard,
blood in ketchup dollops.

Look at em burnin farts,
droppin theyr trousers
to moon at-a camra,
snoggin anyone with genitals
includin the pub mongrel,
puffin like Smokies Corner.

Der! Them bloody teachers,
'ey carn take theyr beer!

## SPIDER IN-A BRIGHT LIGHT

Ring-a ring-a rosies
Pocket fulla posies
Ashes  ashes
Turn to dust!

Sings-a wound up girl
twirlin round-a pole
learnin er toddlin sister
t' swear, er ol man
sits on is 18 pack
swiggin it back
smokin a rollie
"Kayleigh, yew got it wrong...
atishoo it is... Black Death...
they all fell dead, see."

Ee stares at-a spider
an is missis an mate
're all boggly-eyed
as it picks 'cross a web
to-a strugglin fly
over-a bright light.

Kayleigh an is small son
fling bottles o' pop
tryin t' break the web,
ee slurs "Tha's it kids!
Ge' im! Show im wha's what!"

Is little girl come towards im
as ee drains a can, opens another
pours it down er like milk.
The spider retreats, ee olds is ead

as if it'd fall and roll
'long a broken-down bus-station
through puddles o' piss
t' below the brightness
where-a web could stretch.

## SIGNIN F'RA CIRCUS

Seen it in Ponty from-a bus, boyz,
recruitment caravan f'r American army.
Thought I'd join up, see?
I mean, 'ey could send ground troops in,
tha ol Slobberin Milosevic
I'd like t' kick is ead in:
when ee played  f' Villa
I never rated im.

Then I come up to it, boyz,
I seen it wuz f'ra circus.
Bin fooled by-a stars 'n' stripes
an a bloke pointin "We Want You".

So I thought, why not 'en?
People always callin me a clown.
Woman be'ind a counter sayz
"That'll be ten pounds."
"Ten quid t' join a fuckin circus?
Yew gotta be trippin!"

"Oh, you wanna job, do you?"
Starin sif I woz-a Elephant Marn.
"How are you on the trapeze?
Any experience with lions?"

"Well hactulee, I wanna join the army!"
I tol er, puttin er down proper.
An know wha she sayz, boyz?
"Yeah, that's fine by me,
we do need some cannon-fodder."

# MATCHSTICK MAN

Aye, ee were a pucker boxer Johnny,
solid as-a road ee run:
I seen im like a movin skellington,
nose pointin in-a wrong direction.

All them ponces oo complain
don' understand, fightin f' us all ee were.
Grey'ound of a man oo shouldn oughta
ave gone so far, away from-a valley floor
an-a mountain gazin down
at queues o' terraces all expectin.

Subsidence brung im down —
like an ol mine workin, a-ground jes fell
under-a whool town, we staggered
punch-drunk f' months arfta.

Now there's brown boards on-a windows
of-a Matchstick Man, remindin us
of is coffin. I'd batter-a scum
oo stole is mementoes, spewed on is name
like reporters scroungin a story.
I'll always 'member em lines o' people
stretched 'long pavements like ropes o' the ring.

# MAD JACK SPOILS V.E. DAY

We done ower ouse up lovely
like er Ighness woz visitin,
planned to ave a barbeque party
with Fancy Dress wartime clothin.

Not on-a Close isself, mind yew,
this int Balaclava nor Kashmir Street,
we've risen above all that:
jest invited the selected few.

The Murphy's from up-a Close
an-a S4C's down-a way...
didn wan' none o' theyr abuse,
'ey could bugger off f' VE Day.

Wore my dad's ol medals,
my missis woz Vera Lynn,
my boy Ben woz-a SAS corporal,
looked great with is plastic gun.

The bomfire wuz stacked up tidy
like Guy Fawkes all over agen.
Ower guests wuz Churchill, Spitfire pilots, Monty,
neighbours we ardly knew become friends.

Witch 'cross-a street come as a char
(could even stand er voice tha day)
"Appy VD Day!" sayz she with a larf.
"More like Alloween!" I wuz 'bout t' say.

Then in-a jungle eat of-a barbeque
arf-pissed an singin "Slong way t' Tipperary",
'is weird bloke come up t' me,
lookin like ee wuz goin t' spew.

"Yew new round yer?" I ask suspicious.
"I've just returned to peruse the scene."
Ee shot me down with a real posh tone
(SS woz the initials on is fag case).

Ee lit up an I thought "Ow sick!"
"So where have you fought, old man?"
ee queried an I felt like a dick
(neally said The Great Excape pub down town).

Tha's when I knew ee wuz a schizo,
some psycho out on Communitee Care:
babbled on 'bout flingin is medal in-a river
an ow a tank ud soon come by yer.

Ee even talked in bloody Latin,
arpin on 'bout this bloke Owen.
I smiled polite an arst is name,
"Siegfried" ee sayz... might o' known!

I wen' off an let im alone,
friend of-a Murphys most problee,
come t' spoil ower fun: Queen Mum on TV
raisin er and gracious, never armin no-one.

But when-a two minutes silence come
tha total nutter of a man
ee arrives in a stolen tipper truck,
caused chaos, didn give a fuck.

Down ower drive sent tables an buntin flyin,
toppled ower grill yellin 'bout Music Alls.
I phoned 999, tol em an excaped German
wuz on-a loose: 'ey thought I wuz talkin balls.

Mrs Boreman opposite threw frankies at im
like a load-a and grenades aimin,
all-a rest ran in-a ouse shit scared,
I shouted "The police 're comin!" from upstairs.

When ee'd flattened enough, ee went on.
In-a "Merthyr" nex week the eadlines read —
"MAD JACK SPOILS VE DAY CELEBRATIONS!"
Know wha? Ee wuz a soldier oo'd turned out bard!

I reckon them Murphys or Llewellyns ired im,
coz apparently ee ewsed t' write poetree.
An if ee'd bin a soldier surely ee'd-a known
tha all-a tewns 'n' booze 'n' steaks wuz f' victree.

## TOO OL AT FORTY

I kicked-a door in!
Aye, it woz me,
couldn take no more
when-a bossman come on eavy —
treat me like a mat
t' wipe is fancy brogues on.

I swore "Bastard ell!
Leave me be!"
I fel' like cryin,
I fel' like killin im,
is face all smarmy
keeps sayin "Don't need you,
you're a waste of money!"

Coz I'm too ol at forty,
not got enough IT,
far as the net goes
I carn even serve,
ne'mind e-mail
I jest yeard 'bout ET.
Fax? I thought tha woz
another word f'r information,
a desk-top t' me
is where I put my flask on.

I kicked-a door in —
wisht I done it before,
wisht I'd-a grabbed is mobile phone
an rammed it up is jacksy.
Aye, I smashed up-a wood totelee —
trouble is, it woz my own ome!

## LOOK AT ISTREE

"War? What is it good for?
Ab-sol-utely nothin."
I d' love tha song,
but I'll ammer anybody slags off my sister.

An if Kel, oo bothers with me
meets my boyfriend on-a sly,
it'll be worse 'an-a Gulf or Falklands,
my fists'll be atom bombs!

Countrees should know better —
on'y reason we fight
is so we int shat on
or spread like melty butter.

Ow ard yew are, ow soft the others,
tha's all that really matters.
Look at istree: talkin never stopped Itler
an oo tried arguin with Vlad the Impaler?

## A READY TORTURE

Redundancy ewsed t' be
summin never appen t' me.
I got skills, see,
sloggin f'ra Japanese.

Ev'ryone needs videos, TV's,
theyr a way t' get free,
re'glar wages, olidays overseas,
booze t'release me.

Now I'm on death row
waitin t' be tol,
the executioner-boss don' know
ow suff'rin could be so slow,

an ow it feels t' be too old
with all yewr talents sold,
slike a wall with spreadin mould,
roof what don' stop the cold.

Redundancy's a ready torture:
it's the rack o' failure,
ball 'n' chain o' bein a fixture,
compnee-made manacles of-a future.

## GRIM REAPER OF-A FACTREE

Work on-a free samples, mun,
y'know tha stuff come through-a door,
yew on'y try once, skin cream
by mistake yew put on yewr arftas.

Ewsed t' rabbit on 'bout-a Valleys
coolie economy an ow
we woz turnin inta Taiwan,
now that int all theory.

Clock on an off's ol at really,
smore like electronic taggin,
though we int exactly hi-tech
with machinree older 'an my ands.

Don' yer tha no more, d'yew?
But ands is all we are still —
join a Union, don' do no overtime,
too many relatives die, yew'll know.

Tha's when-a Grim Reaper d' come —
we call im tha coz ee lays ands
on any worker don' obey commands.
Off to-a dole cemetree yew go!

Know them plastic sealy bits?
Tha's me, bored shitless,
binocular eyes f' tits
(the missis'd give me a slappin).

Brings in jest enough t' keep
them bailiffs from bootin.
The Grim Reaper earns twice me —
orright f'r im, ee lives in Aberg-bloody-venny!

## ANOTHER BLEEDIN TEAR

Oo come an go
I jes don' know,
in an out an in an out
my mam's a fuckin dog,
she's ooked on Valium
the pills she've popped
t' make er tame.

I carn stand t' listen
when she's back ome
pissed with-a latest one,
'ey groan an moan.
The voices shout em out
urgin me t' break up
ower ouse, ev'ry stone.

Drop tabs, sniff f'r a buzz
anythin t' get outside
t' ride over-a pain.
I spin an spin
in-a big 'all, the tables
an chairs gape an mouth
my name — "Mad Kelly,
wha the ell's she on?"

Desk's a straitjacket,
pen's a needle tranquillisin,
I'm bored bored bored
by fuckin words an questions.
My dad walks past in town
like I woz no-one.
I'm sick o' bangin my ead
'gainst walls, o' cuttin my skin.

The voices get s' loud
they lock ev'ry cell in my brain
"Do this! Do that! Wise up!"

With a splintered club I come
smashin doors an shatterin glass
clearin-a corridors I come
so angry I'd burn down
the whool school with my tongue
"FUCK YEW!" I blister-scream.
Grabbin, throttlin, theyr arms
like belts catchin my limbs.
Calmin words as 'ey pin me to a chair,
talkin o' blame an criminal damage
is all 'ey care: f' ev'ry jagged piece
another bleedin tear.

## ALL AIL OWER BRAN' NEW SYSTEM

## 1

Got more lights 'n Blackpool 'lluminations!
Got more signs 'n Spaghetti Junction!
Fancy routes with numbers
even-a maps don' register,
jest so-a bloody councillors
cun get straight outa town.
Brown eritage places
yew ave t' make appointments
t' visit, like Parry's cottage.

Whool town's like the Church
o' the Present Day Exhaust Fumes,
with Georgetown Villas severed in arf
an Bethesda Street practiclee gone.

An best of all's two footbridges
courtesy of-a Ewropean Communitee,
goin from wasteland t' wasteland,
one a ewge 'A' f'r Arse'oles
(tha's us f' votin them divis in),
even as luminous red 'n' green
stripes, ower night-time attraction.

Roads bindin all o' Merthyr
like Mummy's bandages
embalmed in motor oil.
Roads leadin t' vacant units,
to-a closin-down centre.

## 2

As we woz stuck in-lights I seen im.
Ee jogged 'cross-a junction,
middle-age, baseball cap wrong way round,
walkman eadphones on.

Ee wuz directin all-a traffic,
all-a time movin arms an ands
like some crayzee cop,
this way an that.

When we caught up with im
ee wuz still urryin inta town,
never stopped f'ra green marn,
is ead revolvin a warnin.

If cars ud followed is ands
they'd be in-a river upside down,
or skewed 'cross verges, growlin
like muzzled Rottweilers.

## WAITIN T' BE ROBBED

Come up yer, top o' the ill
posh ouse, even-a bird-box
ave got 'n extension!
Gotta new job, see,
in-a ewge fancy factree,
ad enough o' that estate,
they'd take yew bloody bin
few leave it out late.

Come up yer, as I say
to executive, detached Beacon 'eights,
tidy view o' the mountains
(pity 'bout a gas-tank though),
even gotta kiddies playground
what don' look like a skip.

Come up yer, outa the way
o' them gangs o' scruffians,
lager louses an tarty girls
oo scream like rollercoasters
an what appens, would yew b'lieve?
5 metres from ower back fence,
near as yew'd jump practiclee —
they wanna dig it up!

Seen it all f' the first time —
nex to-a stables, to-a swings,
right nex to-a local,
they'd ave a great big ole.
Seen it like I'd bin blind —
the ramblin eather, wild flowers
growin ev'rywhere an-a bracken
like the illside's air.

It wuz jest like some gang
in offices threatnin, but-a law
couldn do nothin. We woz elpless
as ol folks stuck in flats
theyer windows bein stoned —
waitin f' lorries an JCB's,
waitin t' be robbed of ower ealth
an peace an a steady ome.

## COULDA BIN SUMMIN

So wha's appnin an wha's news?
Think yew know me, yew an yew an yew?
Seen me on yewer tellies
pushin-a trolley, with a big belly.
Seen-a statistics, igh-rise flats,
them politicians makin stabs
at girls like me livin on ower own.
Few could see me, yew'd problee moan —
"Tart! Slag! Scrubber! Dog!"
Blonde frizz, scarlet lips, the whool og.
But I don' friggin care no more
coz what 'bout im openin-a door,
enterin an leavin is stain on-a floor
f' me t' mop up on my knees...
yew'd say I led im on, teased
an dangled-a key before is nose
(still got is mess on my clothes).

Yew stare at me, the tight fit
an yew int seen nothin, right?
Coz I ewsed t' be so tidy
a real swot stuck in nightly
makin words 'n' figures join
like wall-tiles an jest as borin,
botherin on'y with A-type kids
an collectin posters o' Ryan Giggs.
Knew where I wuz goin, see:
tanned as a poster in a Travel Agency.

My parents ardly thought o' my intentions.
I coulda bin a roof-space or an extension
that needed fixin, they wuz too preoccupied
workin all owers, livin t' buy

the ouse before they died.
I could take-a jip I ad off rebels
seen em actin big, chokin like fools
as 'ey dragged in bogs, splutterin stink,
didn wanna grow ol in a blink.
Till Dean come along, lush an knowin,
like I looked out sudden, seen-a town
not jest streets named arfta dead celebritees:
when ee smiled I felt really free.
Ee wern no divi neither,
pen to im woz a brush to painter.
Tol me t' wise up, be young
before-a world would be ung
with-a noose of ower atmosphere:
all this wuz on'y films before.

So I tore up my Man. U. posters
tatooed Dean across my laughter;
but I still couldn follow im,
knew my parents watched all-a time.
Scared I woz, arfta years inside:
flowers on my bedrooms walls ud lied.

I could see Dean struttin away
leavin me in a window-frame,
could imagine im in a bus-shelter
makin some other girl warm as fur.
When my dad sayz "Tha Dean's a waster!
Comes from the Gurnos. Family o' gypos!"
I jest knew I ad t' go
to-a bench where 'ey all met:
offered fags an cider, I didn regret,
but drew in smoke, acted mean.
Yew shoulda seen-a face on Dean!
From 'en on, one thing arfta another,

so many roads I ad to discover.
Best of all woz is parents bed,
we bonked away till raw red.
When ee'd come an leave me early
it wern tha much of a party.

Soon I wuz late an feelin sick
as an angover, is prick
jabbed at me sharp an sore,
I turned away an yeard is anger
"Ow could I be such a dick?"
"So now yew gonna leave?"
Ee sayz "No way!" an "Love, love..."
groanin like ee ad some disease.

I arf believed im, ee made plans f'ra boy:
buy im a small motorbike, all kinda toys.
My dad ee spat ev'ry word at me
"Go an ave yewr little gypo in a field!"
My mam tol me to go, wuz ol enough
"Yew've made yewr bed, my girl... Tough!"
She couldn face-a neighbours talkin,
'ey woz smarmy to er face with "Pooer Siân!
Thought she'd do well, get a proper career.
Tha young man's trouble, I'm shewer."
When 'ey flung me out I wuz goin spare,
Dean promised stuff, but didn care.
I wuz already one too many,
ee wuz always gazin away
at posin girls with slim bodies.

Tha's why I'm bunged up yer now
in 'n SS Guest Ouse, feelin like a cow
on'y good f' milkin in chains:
the bull gets in now an agen

to ave is rent, to ave is way.
I carn get out, don' wanna stay.

Dean wen' off, leavin me crawlin,
beggin a Ousin t' give me 'ccomodation.
While ee goes cavortin round-a pubs
an untin f' other girls in-a clubs,
I'm in 'is piss-pot cell an-a jailer
is-a landlord oo'd ave me wander
to and fro down-a streets makin money
from ev'ry angin perve, f'on'y I'd agree.

If I sayz "Bugger off, yew turd. Go 'way!"
ee takes is rent with-a butcherin pain.
My walls 're grey as barred metal,
but if I sol' is white pills
ee'd paint em colour of a weddin.
Wouldn be seen dead peddlin tha poison.

My baby'll be born f'ra kill,
ee reaches up to it, clampin me still.
There are others yer worse off:
girls ee ewses t' bribe-a cops,
an boyz ee've ad chopped
f' nickin stuff 'ey shoulda sold.
Livin yer I 've grown old
by-a second, saggin an suffocatin
as ee sayz "Siân! Yew coulda bin summin!"

PEOPLE YEW DON' SEE

We're people yew don' see,
we're the invisible people,
ones yew turn out t' be
no matter ow careful.

We got clothes fit f'ra Jumble,
buy cans o' meat an cheap bread,
we obble off of the buses
weighed down by ower debt.

We're those yew don' want t' know,
bein old jest isn't the thing:
ow many newsreaders on telly,
ow many soap stars cun yew name?

Soon yew'll pack us away
to some nice shut-up Ome
called Daffodils or Sunny View:
on'y ower memrees free t' roam.

Wrinkles, grey air an shrinkin,
joints what do rust like a car,
we scrabble off-a paltry pension,
the pain-killers never go far.

We are the invisible ewmans
remindin ow close yew are
to the cemetrees an the Crem.,
t' the earth an also the fire.

NEW AGE RIOT

We ad it all sorted,
even-a name.

We ad exercise books
full o' lyrics,
good stuff an all
with loadsa language.

I woz-a bassist
though I adn learnt yet,
Ash woz on lead
an ee could play a bit.
We had a drummer,
but no drum kit.

We ad all-a best influences
from Nirvana t' the Manics.
Ash ud even designed
ower first album cover,
with the devil umpin a sheep.

We wuz gunna be so sick
we'd make-a Sex Pistols
seem like-a Bee Gees,
we'd expose owerselfs
on primetime TV.

We woz so close
the boyz called us "bum chums" —
I think tha got to im.
An when ee tol me
ee wuz seein Mandy Goth
I larfed, thought ee wuz piss-takin.
Ee slapped me real ard,

broken nose, black eye, the lot.
We split before we could start,
least I did anyway,
totelee mashed up my face
like the Oo with theyr guitars.
The end o' my rock career,
though ee'd problee end up in Oasis.

## BANNED

Whappnin Gaj mun,
whappnin son!

I'm gaspin Gaj,
got a rollie?
Skin up 'en.

Goin t' the match, mun,
ope I get in.
I wuz banned, Gaj,
away at Luton,
cops found a can,
tol em where t' stick it.
Theyr fans burned-a Dragon
an 'ey didn do nothin!

Like my disguise, mun?
Cap wrong way round,
better still no booze,
see my ands, no shakin.

Sall I care 'bouts gettin in —
when we chant, Gaj,
I'm outa my skin
an when we score
I'm flyin so igh.
When we lose I'm down
grubbin f' stub-ends.

## SOAP STAR

Well, she've made it
an good f'r er,
she've got the readies
an a bran' new car.

We made a bit an all,
'ey took ower ouse over,
tha's why we d' watch ev'ry week,
t' see ower furniture.

Course she've done great,
aye, fair's fair:
though all she've done so far
is stand an stare.

See, trouble is they're sayin
there's larfin or moany famlees,
but the truth int like tha:
wha's left of-a communitee?

On'y las week 'is ol fella died
oo lived up by yer,
nobody'd ardly seen im,
ee adn bin out f' years.

Well, I carn deny she've made it
an ev'ryone wan's t' be on telly,
but as far as I cun see
it's jest like any industree.

It's figures what they want
an I s'pose she've got one now,
but wait till they d' drop:
don' think 'ey'll ewse er some'ow.

## PASSION FRUIT

Ee'd shag anythin.
Not anythin as in sheep,
or even anythin as in
two legs standin or lyin.
But anythin as in THING!

Ee begun modest like,
avin wallets an purses,
but turnin vegetarian
ee acquired a likin
f' vegetables an fruit.
Oranges woz reluctant
an stung is ol boy,
kiwis tended t' fall off
at the crucial moment.

But melons... they woz
is on'y true valentines.
Oneydew, Skin o' the frog,
ee adored theyer lastin
Mediterranean passions.

Ee'd spend owers
'long the soopermarket shelves
sniffin an feelin
f'r the right one.
One day ee ad
a really big watermelon,
never got t' the main course,
starters turned im on.

Aye, ee'd shag anythin,
till ee experimented

with a pomegranate
an all them seeds
ad t' be surgically extracted
from under is skin!

# JITTERBUG JADE

Ambushin-a buses
openin 'mergency boxes
makin ice balls
t' fling at teachers' cars
twirlin gum on one finger
slaggin off-a swots
from-a pissin bus-shelter

run on-a bus
never sit down
swing on-a pole
an ring t' ring
yell an squeal
crunch on crisps
gulp back red pop
driver shouts — "Yew wanna walk?"

rush up 'n' down
give a big burp
larf at Stace, Lynz an Don
as 'ey press lips t' windows
at a gel-boyz passin

"Jade! Jade! Jitterbug Jade!"
my mam do say,
"yew're totelee yper!
Too many E's!"
But I int ad any,
my step-dad sayz
"She mus be on speed!"

## THE BIG OLE

When-a Council sold
the Big Ole f'ra quid
t' turn into a ewge tip
oo'da believed it?

When-a litter wuz carried
by a breeze all over
the footie an rugby fields,
so they wuz giant bins

an it wuz mingin strong
as them chemical weapons,
we coughed an muttered —
oo'da thought it mattered?

When-a gas come right up
from-a sewers an children
spewed theyer guts out,
oo wuz askin-a questions?

When-a froth begun t' ooze
from-a nearby drains,
it wuz like-a tip spreadin
poison tentacles round us.

"Landfill tax!" the councillors cried,
"look what it ave give us."
All em back'anders an bribes,
but no cure f' daily sickness.

## NO FASHION ON A PLATE

I got it all —
a future in coll.,
boyfren oo's mega-lush,
famlee oo've shown
wha's right, wha's wrong.

I got it all —
eczam certificates
an piano grades,
fren's oo ave a larf,
even teachers oo talk
t' me one-t'-one.

I got it all —
'cept the mirror
tells the truth
(scales lie on my be'alf).
The mirror shames me,
a fairground freak.

I got nothin at all —
the food is poison
longin t' choke,
t' strangle my guts,
t' fill me fat.
I read out recipes
an 'ey smell o' puke.

I got nothin at all —
owever many times
they call me "petite"
I know ow quick
them bulges inflate

so's I look like a toad
puffed an obscene —
no fashion on a plate.

## SMELLY SHELLY

"Smelly Shelly!" they d' call me
even though I'm ol enough
to ave a famlee:
the name's stuck
like dogshit to a mat.

An I know 'ey never
bin learnt t' me,
them simple basics
like full-stops an commas:
ow t' wash under yewr arm-pits.

I'm run off-of my feet
lookin arfta four little ones
as my mam works
er balls off (if she ad any)
t' pay f'r ower keep.

An Drama's ev'rythin t' me,
don' care if it's Russell or Delaney,
I cun be oo I wanna be,
dress s' they carn see
an when 'ey clap, it's "Never Shelly!"

TROLLEY PUSH
(i.m. Phyllis Evans)

We woz down by C'filly
so's not t' be known,
though-a Red Choir wuz singin,
so they musta guessed
tha summin wuz goin on.

There wuz two couples, yewr son,
yew an yewr good friend.
We all wen in t' gether,
nothin like skillful plannin!
Still, it wuz a change from leaflettin:
ower anti-market stand
an comments like — "Quite right,
I wouldn buy nothin touched by blacks!"

My kids thought it woz great
fillin ower trolley with loadsa cans,
spyin at labels, Cape produce,
they musta made more noise
than a chantin demo 'long the aisles.

Yew an yewr friend swanned past
pickin an choosin, in no rush.
Before-a checkout we'd all bin ad,
securitee stoppin ower trolleys.

None of em suspected two ol ladies
an ev'rythin wen through-a till,
can arfta can o' veg an fruit
an two bars o' chocolate
mos problee made in York.
"Don' wan them cans," yew said,

"they're S. African.We're anti-apartheid.
We'll ave the chocolate instead."

I'll never forget tha manager
tellin securitee t' throw yew out,
swear ee'd seen Nelson Mandela,
Maggie's terrorist visitin is store.